DREAM COTTAGES

DREAM COTTAGES

KATIE ELLIS

83
PRESS

Hoffman Media
2323 2nd Avenue North
Birmingham, AL 35203
hoffmanmedia.com

83
PRESS®

ISBN #979-8-9874820-1-8
Printed in China

TABLE OF CONTENTS

D. PORTHAULT
THE ART OF
LUXURY LINENS

DAVID MONN

INTRODUCTION

What is a dream cottage? To some, it may look like a charming historic home filled with vintage treasures. Perhaps it's a sweet little retreat nestled somewhere along the coast or in an idyllic neighborhood. To others, that dream may be a newly built or renovated home with modern cottage amenities that serves as a special place to gather with family and friends. Our team of editors at *The Cottage Journal* magazine knows that dream homes can come in all different sizes and styles. We've compiled this inspired collection of 15 dream-worthy spaces that showcase diverse designs.

Our featured interior designers and homeowners from across the country invite us into these real homes and share their distinctive style ideas and decorating tips. Each home holds special stories that highlight treasured collections, influential travels, long-awaited renovations, growing families, and of course, the thoughtful blending of old and new décor.

To us, cottage style goes beyond an architectural or design element—it's a relaxed elegance and layered with charm. Nothing feels too opulent or precious, and every space is meant to be fully lived in and enjoyed. We hope that within the pages of this extraordinary collection of homes, you discover design ideas that resonate with your unique tastes and find inspiration to create your own spaces that are not only lovely but personal.

CLASSIC COTTAGES

FROM THE VINTAGE CHARM OF HISTORIC HOMES TO THE MODERN
AMENITIES OF CONTEMPORARY DESIGNS, OUR CLASSIC COTTAGES
HIGHLIGHT SOPHISTICATED STYLE MEANT FOR RELAXED LIVING.

Twist on Traditional Style

BOLD COLORS AND EXCITING PATTERNS REIGN SUPREME IN THIS HISTORIC COTTAGE.

Homeowner Liz Morrow isn't afraid of color or pattern. So, when she and her husband, Craig, moved into their English Tudor-style cottage in Dallas, Texas, they were eager to embrace traditional style in a way that felt fresh and contemporary. To help bring their vision to life, the couple called on interior designer Kim Armstrong. Kim is also an enthusiast of eclectic, colorful interiors, so she and Liz made a perfect pair on this project.

The historic home was originally designed by famed architect Charles Dilbeck, and when the Morrows purchased the house, it still held all its original hand-carved woodwork details and custom ironworks throughout, including the ornate staircase railings, chandeliers, and hardware on the doors. "[The house] had great bones, and we wanted to glorify that," Kim says. "[Liz] loves color—that was the driving force—so we had to use color and pattern in a way that would not distract from the architecture but would enhance the space."

13

A vibrant pop of red on the exterior front door welcomes guests with a preview of the visual treat that awaits inside. The foyer area opens into a cathedral-style vaulted ceiling in the formal living room, where the original woodwork and iron chandelier immediately draw the eyes upward. Kim worked with Liz to tastefully furnish the room with a mix of antique finds and repurposed pieces. They reviewed hundreds of fabric samples to create a custom, cohesive look. "[Liz] would pick the things that really spoke to her, and then based on that, I would build the design concept around what she gravitated towards," Kim says. "The driving forces were Brunschwig & Fils and Schumacher fabrics. You'll see a lot of that being used in the space."

Comfortable, colorful seating areas continue into the den. A pair of reupholstered Bergère chairs pop in a pink Peter Fasano fabric. "He's got fabulous prints and bright colors and more of a traditional design," Kim says. "So, it was a great fit for this [room]!"

While Kim sourced many new pieces for this lively Southern charmer, she also reused and repurposed some of Liz's existing pieces. In the dining room, she reupholstered the chairs in Schumacher's Chiang Mai Dragon fabric in blue and stripped the original mahogany stain to create a more weathered look to match the antique dining table.

Playful patterns and bold colors seem to blend effortlessly from room to room. While it takes a trained eye and years of experience to master this style, Kim says her baseline tip for mixing color and pattern is to always pair organic and geometric shapes, which helps create a visual balance. "Pull colors from your inspiration and change up the scale [of patterned prints]," Kim says. "A lot of people think you have to go 'matchy-matchy,' but if there's blue, blue blends and works beautifully with so many differing shades of blues. You don't have to be consistent with one exact shade; I actually think it adds more interest when you vary the shades a little bit."

The dining room ceiling highlights the home's beautiful original woodwork and unique architecture. "We really wanted to glorify that," Kim says. "We didn't want to add anything that was going to distract—but [Liz] loves pattern and color. So, it was doing that in a smart way that would elevate the design."

Each of the home's four bedrooms takes on its own unique personality—and all are expertly layered with a merry mix of patterns. One of Kim's favorite bedrooms to design was a nursery for the Morrows' grandchildren. "They knew they were going to be grandparents, and they really wanted to create a space for everyone to feel comfortable when they came to visit," Kim says. The wallpapered sloped walls give the room an attic-like feel that is sweetly serene. In addition to playing with patterns, Kim also suggests giving your eyes a place to rest. "So, even with a busy [guest] bedroom, with the toile [pattern] on the walls and the ceiling wallpapered, I did white bedding," she says. "And that's my place for the eyes to rest."

Faced with so many brilliant colors and unique antique finds, it's hard not to smile inside this cozy cottage. "This project was fun because [Liz] loves antiques. She's not scared of color, and she's not scared of pattern. . . . When I think we've gone over the top, [Liz would] say, 'What about wallpapering the ceiling?'" Kim says. "Her fearless boldness in selection really elevated the project even more!"

Liz's design style is foundationally traditional, and her use of fresh, colorful prints gives it a contemporary twist.

With the growing popularity of grandmillennial style, antiques are once again finding a time to shine. "This project came about during the height of mid-century modern [design popularity]," Kim says. "So, I was super excited with this house. It was really fun to shop for all the antiques!"

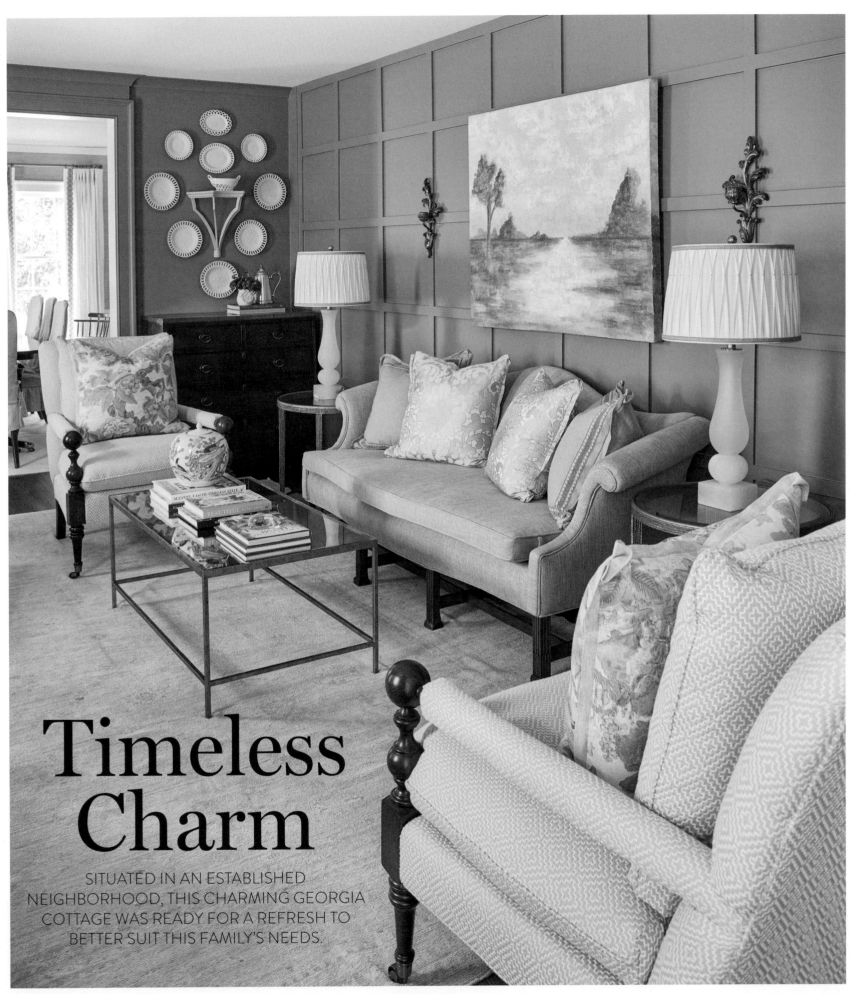

Timeless Charm

SITUATED IN AN ESTABLISHED
NEIGHBORHOOD, THIS CHARMING GEORGIA
COTTAGE WAS READY FOR A REFRESH TO
BETTER SUIT THIS FAMILY'S NEEDS.

After raising three daughters in their well-appointed home in Atlanta, the homeowners called on interior design expert Maggie Griffin to help update and reclaim their space as they found themselves in an exciting new phase of life with adult children and young grandchildren.

"We used a lot of their existing pieces," Maggie says. "We were able to freshen things up with new fabrics and re-cover [well-loved pieces]." The design team made great use of the family's collections and furnishings, so while nearly every surface was touched and the home feels new, it also has some age and special character to it.

Double doors open into the foyer, which welcomes guests into this timeless Southern home. A beautiful grass cloth wall covering from Schumacher gives an elevated touch that perfectly pairs with the blue-and-white chinoiserie-style lamps and handsome antique console. An elegant runner underfoot adds warmth and beckons you further inside.

Through the entry, you step up into the formal living room. "I love that immediately when you walk in, it feels like the house has been there for a long time and like things have been added over time," Maggie says.

To refresh this space, the design team worked in tandem with the builder and homeowners. The builder added custom millwork along one wall, which makes for a stunning visual accent, and the entire room got a fresh coat of paint in Antique Pewter by Benjamin Moore. "It's this great kind of steely gray that looks green or blue or gray, depending on the light," Maggie says. The camelback sofa and skirted club chairs were family pieces that got a new life thanks to fresh upholstery, while a pair of brand-new side chairs and an updated coffee table create a lovely balance of old and new.

Just steps beyond the living area awaits an intimate dining room for family gatherings. "It's not a large space, but [the homeowners] genuinely spend a lot of family meals there, and I think that's really lovely because a

lot of people don't actually use their dining rooms," Maggie says. The champagne-blush-colored grass cloth wall covering and crystal chandelier set the tone for a sweetly feminine space, and a pretty screen doubles as artwork. The table and chairs were original to the homeowners. "We created slipcovers on the chairs, which is one of my favorite ways to keep something from feeling old or stodgy," Maggie says. "We also re-covered the seats of the chairs underneath those slipcovers, so [the wife] essentially has two different chairs where she could use the slipcovers or not."

The design team worked with skilled craftsmen to combine the existing kitchen with another smaller room to give the homeowners one large kitchen with an eat-in island, a breakfast nook, and keeping room. "We built a white kitchen that felt very natural for them because it does read so cottage. It's very classic," Maggie says. The use of high-quality materials like quartz countertops, a Wolf range, and panel-ready appliances help to create that seamless look. Maggie incorporated plenty of seating areas between the island and the adjoining keeping room. "The four chairs [by the fireplace] were really important to the homeowner because it was a perfect little spot to sit with her three girls," Maggie says.

The paneled study is the heart of the home and serves as a cozy retreat for the couple to relax. Maggie's team re-covered and repurposed their existing furniture, which helped to make everything feel fresh. And they displayed the husband's collection of antique duck decoys using a stylish bracket under each. "It doesn't distract from the television wall and is more artful," she says.

Just beyond the eat-in island, the keeping room offers a comfortable seating area by the fireplace. A cozy breakfast table and chairs find a home near the window, creating a perfect place for casual dining. And pretty drapery adds a relaxed softness and warmth to the all-white kitchen.
Opposite: A collection of green majolica plates are artfully hung above a chest in the hallway near the stairwell. "These were pieces that [the homeowner] had that we just hung in a new, fresh way," Maggie says.

In the study, Maggie created a wet bar with a hard-wearing black granite countertop that can withstand pretty much anything. Above it, the husband's antique collection doubles as artwork. "He has this beautiful extensive collection of antique soldiers that are part of his family heirlooms, and we wanted to highlight those but not in a juvenile way," Maggie says. "So, I had acrylic boxes built for them to house his soldier collection, and I think it's just a really artful way that we displayed a very important collection with a modern twist."

Opposite: The hall bath is filled with cottage-style details. Dark hardwood floors contrast with the creamy white beaded board and decorative wallpaper above. A café curtain adds a soft touch with a lively pattern while newly added cabinetry and countertops give the room a fresh look.

Two of their adult daughters live in town, so the couple didn't necessarily need dedicated bedrooms for them anymore. "[The homeowners] needed more sophisticated guest bedrooms," Maggie says. "That was important for us to make [the rooms] feel kind of gender neutral and not so specific to [their] girls." Soft and stylish, the guest bedrooms utilize as many family pieces possible, and one now doubles as a nursery for visiting grandchildren.

In addition to a full home interior refresh, the couple was also ready to invest in their personal space with a primary suite addition that included a dreamy bedroom and bathroom, complete with his-and-hers closets as well as a home office.

"Because of the way the roofline was hitting the existing part of the house, we could gain that extra head height, which I think makes such a difference," Maggie says. "The rest of the house has 8-foot ceilings, and then, you walk in there, and it's just beautiful." Incorporating tongue-and-groove woodwork to the ceiling added cottage-style interest and texture overhead.

The design team accentuated the dramatic scale of the newly added room with a beautiful chandelier from Visual Comfort, big mirrors above large nightstands, and a soft bound carpet underfoot. The homeowners requested a design scheme that was "updated traditional," which translated to new linens, a pleated bed skirt, and heavy drapery. "It's got a very grandmillennial vibe," Maggie says. "We've got the very soft cottage feel."

Moving into the primary bathroom, they had the opportunity for a wow factor. A pretty white marble contrasts with soft gray accents, and a built-in seat beneath a window with a café curtain adds to the sweet Southern style. "This bathroom is not huge, but it has some very clever storage solutions," Maggie says. "We really utilized everything we could to maximize the space and give [the homeowners] storage."

The new bathroom addition boasts clever storage solutions. The builder created a designated space for the homeowner to do her makeup, and instead of holding a small center drawer, the cabinet lifts up to provide a built-in mirror. "I think that's very smart," Maggie shares. And the cabinet tower in the corner was built to hold all kinds of extra products.

The addition thoughtfully considered the connection to the outdoors. The couple's dreamy bedroom opens to the screened back porch. They chose a beautiful stone for the floor and sourced stylish, durable furniture from Summer Classics that makes outdoor living an absolute delight. The scene is complete with a porch swing bed, a large grill, and a wood-burning fireplace. "Having the screen makes it more [accessible] year-round in the South," Maggie says.

Packed with personal character and timeless charm, this newly renovated cottage-style retreat is now ready for a new phase of life for the growing family who lives there.

A Personal Canvas

A DALLAS, TEXAS, DESIGNER PUTS HER DISTINCTIVE MARK ON HER HISTORIC COTTAGE, PRESERVING ITS CLASSIC ARCHITECTURAL ALLURE WHILE INFUSING THE INTERIORS WITH A MIX OF STYLES ALL HER OWN.

When Emily Johnston Larkin of EJ Interiors discovered her 1926 English Tudor-style cottage in the historic Lakewood neighborhood of Dallas, Texas, the curb appeal was undeniable. Built by Dines & Kraft Building Company, notable developers of the early 1900s, the home's striking rooflines, picturesque brick and stonework, and expansive stained-glass bay windows imbue instant enchantment. And though the interior was filled with equally impressive architectural character, Emily and her husband, Ben, immediately began plans for a multiphase renovation that would preserve its original charm while creating a functional space for their growing family—as well as a beautiful backdrop for Emily's dynamic style.

"We bought the home in 2018 knowing we would need more space and then moved out for an extensive yearlong overhaul in 2019," Emily says. "The home works for us because the front still has the original formal spaces, which we wanted to preserve, and then the renovated rooms at the back encompass modern-day living with an open kitchen and family room concept. My vision was to stay true to the architectural style of the home. I didn't want our addition to be an obvious one and wanted it to flow seamlessly with what was built in the 1920s."

Opposite: The home's stunning showcase of historic architectural features begins with distinction in the entryway, where designer Emily Johnston Larkin enriched original elements like "Morning Tile" and stained glass with a framed vintage Gracie wallpaper panel as well as personal pieces like love letters that her grandmother wrote to her grandfather.

They worked to perfect the new floor plan with construction designer Carol Gantt of Gantt Design, who specializes in the renovations of historic Lakewood homes, updating the kitchen, family room, and primary and powder bathrooms while also building out the attic space to create another bedroom with an en suite bath, a nursery, and a playroom. With the additions, they made sure to incorporate architectural repetition, mimicking structural elements like the original arched doorways.

Emily says what makes this home so unique at the foundational level is how many of its original features remain intact, from the 1920s "Morning Tile" that greets you in the entryway, harmonizing with the architecturally notable fireplace and mantel tiling just beyond, to the ornate plaster molding that makes its way around the formal living area and into the dining room.

"We even removed all of the molding in my living room when we took out the ceilings and then reinstalled it at the end of the project," Emily says. "Keeping the historic aspects of the home was really important to us—no matter what lengths we had to go to preserve it." She then contrasted these elaborate original embellishments like the crown molding and stained glass with more transitional furnishings, such as contemporary wing chairs and a sofa with track arms and a waterfall skirt.

"I didn't want my home to feel stuffy and too traditional, so the addition of more modernized pieces gives it some tension and balance," Emily says. "I used classic materials that gave a nod to the Tudor style of the home with a hint of Art Deco. My house is very much a traditional cottage, but with updated details to keep it looking young and fresh. I love a sense of history and only like to incorporate art that is meaningful," she says of pieces like the framed love letters penned by her grandparents that grace the living room alongside abstract works. "I really strive to achieve a juxtaposition of old and new."

When it came to color, Emily utilized Benjamin Moore's White Dove as a base and enlivened it with plenty of soft notes of pastel, as well as vibrant artwork, fun fabrics, and even a few bold wall coverings. "I consider blue a neutral, so I used blue in almost every room," she says, referencing a specific icy shade she chose. "I carried this hue throughout for some consistency, but I didn't want a blue-and-white house, so in each room, I have accent colors to break up the monotony and add contrast."

The dining room and kitchen tout the most dedicated blue-and-white schemes, but with a juxtaposed approach. The more saturated dining room bears a vintage Schumacher wallpaper that feels at once whimsical and classic as it coalesces with collected china and chinoiserie, while the kitchen employs a crisp white aesthetic with coordinating accents across the blue-green spectrum.

Emily carried the dining room's Schumacher wallpaper into the stairwell that the space opens up to. An original archway connects the dining room to the living room, and an indistinguishable replica crafted during the renovation graces the opening that adjoins the kitchen.

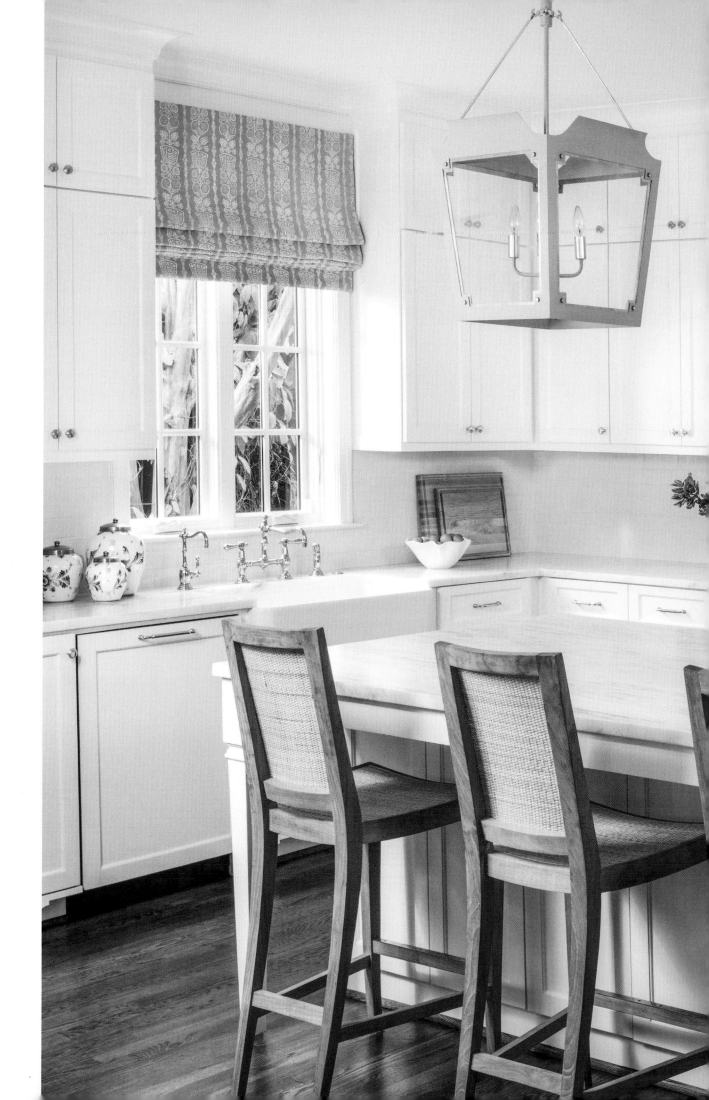

"I think white is so classic in a kitchen, and I didn't want to do anything too trendy in here in terms of paints or stain," Emily says. She enlivened the blank slate with a blue-and-white Roman shade, celadon green lantern pendant lights, and a few curated accents spanning artwork and ceramics.

The upstairs additions continue the calming pastel palette, from Emily's signature ice blue on the guest room walls to a pink floral paper in the nursery paired with sentimental art, such as a portrait of Emily's grandmother. These former attic spaces highlight their original rooflines and previously hidden architectural features like stained-glass windows above the bathroom's claw-foot tub, achieving distinctive character and cozy charm.

Emily's personality shines throughout the home's timeless foundation with thoughtful details tucked into every corner—details the designer says are always evolving. "Making decisions for your own home is much more difficult than working on a client's home," Emily says. "I see so many beautiful things on a daily basis that it becomes hard to commit to a fabric or wallpaper, and I strive to never use the same material twice to make each project one of a kind. I consider my house my laboratory where I can experiment with new ideas, but that also gets me into trouble as things are always changing around here."

The nursery makes the most of the quirky rooflines that resulted from its attic-space origins, using them to create cozy nooks for a crib and a rocker. The renovation team knocked out a stone element on the exterior façade to construct the porthole window above the crib. "I put an antique sunburst mirror around it that happened to fit perfectly," Emily says. Continuing the thread of meaningful artwork woven throughout the abode, a sketch of Emily's grandmother who modeled for Neiman Marcus in the 1950s keeps company with an abstract of Lake Como, a family-favorite travel destination—as well as the room's contribution to the home's recurrent ice-blue hue.

A Change of Space

A LITTLE OLD, A LITTLE NEW, AND A LOT OF CREATIVITY TURNED OUT TO BE THE PERFECT RECIPE FOR THIS COTTAGE REDESIGN.

It began with the need for a refresh. The 1930s cottage in the Collier Hills neighborhood of Atlanta, Georgia, while filled with beloved treasures, needed an update to tone down the colorful palette into something more serene. "She loves antiques, she loves collections, and she's got a lot of beautiful things," says designer Anna-Louise Wolfe of the homeowner, who wanted a more neutral setting in which to display her treasures. But even in the updates, Anna-Louise sought to preserve the integrity and age of the house, maintaining the cottage charm that was so integral to its spirit.

Rather than starting fresh, Anna-Louise's approach was to edit the homeowner's existing pieces, then design each space around the most loved selections. In the living room, a pair of French wingback chairs in Brunschwig & Fils fabric informed the new selections. "Those were the focal point in there," Anna-Louise says. Working with the existing collection of black chinoiserie, she sourced pieces like an antique hot water urn, which she had converted into a lamp for a new take on an aged element. "I was rearranging, repurposing, and kind of switching things up, but [the homeowner] was a collector herself, so she already had such beautiful antiques," she says.

Because the previous owners had made updates to the kitchen, the team found they only needed to freshen it up with touches like paint and new hardware, as well as a quaint floral fabric skirt over a storage cubby. Similarly, the dining room makeover consisted mostly of refreshing the homeowner's existing dining set, which she had found at an estate sale some years earlier. "But just to breathe a little bit of new life into the Queen Anne chairs . . . I had my faux painter paint them," Anna-Louise notes.

In addition to collected treasures, the design also incorporated passed-down family pieces like a set of quilt blocks stitched by a late relative. "They were quilting samplers of her trying out different stitches with different fabrics—just practicing before making the actual quilt," Anna-Louise says. She had them framed and hung in the den, where they serve as both artwork and a conversation starter. "So, those were the focal point in there that we pulled the colors from and then tried to keep everything else neutral so that they would really stand out."

Pulling its color scheme from the framed quilt blocks on the wall, the den uses a beige backdrop to offset a richer palette of reds and blacks. "I think it just adds depth to a room to have some black in it," Anna-Louise notes.

A gallery wall in the home office displays a collection of works painted by the homeowner's father. "We kind of went through and edited and picked favorites," Anna-Louise says. Beneath them, a pair of lamps converted from antique candelabras show off the creative approach to this design process. Anna-Louise admits they're one of her favorite parts of the new design. "Those were something that I picked out for her, to be the statement in that room," she adds. A French sofa upholstered in blue and white remained untouched, though Anna-Louise recovered the chairs in the room to better pair with it.

Rather than drawing from an heirloom or piece of art, like so many of the rooms in the home did, the primary bedroom instead found inspiration in a beloved print—Bowood by Cowtan & Tout. "When we were talking about what [the homeowner] wanted, she said, 'I don't want anything too fussy or floral, except I've always loved Bowood,'" says Anna-Louise, who was delighted to incorporate the print that had long been a personal favorite. They selected a linen version that felt, as she puts it, "a little bit more casual and updated than the old-school formal chintz," and paired it with a complementary gingham, both of which repeat across the space in multiple spots. "I think bedrooms need to be more serene and kind of quieter," says Anna-Louise. "So, I feel like when you stick with the same repeating pattern, it's calmer and more soothing."

The connected bathroom needed more work than much of the rest of the home, as it was covered in outdated green tile—likely added in the 1980s. The good news was that it was a fun place to play with the finishing touches, which Anna-Louise says often go unnoticed or underappreciated. "I would say one of the fun things about this client was that she loves detail," Anna-Louise says. Touches like the scalloped edges found on the shower curtain and Roman window shade show off the thoughtfulness of the design and highlight both women's appreciation for the little things.

More repeating patterns appear in the guest bedroom, which utilizes bolder shades of aqua and vibrant greens. At the request of the homeowner, Anna-Louise incorporated the headboard and a Victorian settee at the foot of the bed, which were formerly a heavy, dark wood. "These were both pieces that were things she had from her family or collected when she was young, and so, she wasn't fully ready to get rid of them," she says. "And since it was the bedroom, and we were using this really beautiful, bold floral, I didn't really feel the need to mix another strong pattern with it—I just kind of let the floral be the showstopper piece."

New paint and fabric reinvented family pieces in the guest bedroom, where scattered antique accessories add character and personal history throughout. "[The homeowner] had very unique things that I would just try to use in different ways and kind of breathe new life into them," says Anna-Louise. A subdued green shade on the walls was the perfect choice for showing off bold florals and creating a sense of calm.

The screened porch captures Anna-Louise's approach to the design, pairing the beauty of existing pieces with new additions that both complement and elevate them. "She had this antique wicker that was still in good condition and just needed to be repainted," she says. With a bit of fresh paint and new upholstery, the sitting area took on a new life. While the dining chairs did need to be replaced, they selected a set that matched the existing furniture—though they opted to replace the previous table with an antique pine table that creates a charming contrast. "We just kind of warmed it up a little by adding the natural element of having that pine color out there," she adds.

From the foyer to the porch, the redesign not only preserved the homeowner's most cherished collections, but it implemented creative techniques to show them in a fresh light. With a new, neutral palette and updated touches that honor the history of the home, Anna-Louise helped the most special elements in this cottage stand out in the very best way.

Well-Crafted Cottage

THIS CRAFTSMAN-STYLE HOME GAINED SQUARE FOOTAGE WITHOUT LOSING ITS SOUL.

When a husband and wife decided to expand their Arlington, Virginia, house to accommodate their growing family, they didn't want to forgo intimacy for scale. With two school-age kids, the homeowners' desire for a warm, comfortable house was key.

"The expanded layout of the renovated house, with its second-story addition, was driven by a familiar goal: to create open, definable yet welcoming spaces for the family to gather for living and dining. The elimination of the walls that once separated these functions into isolated spaces also creates continuity," says Charles Moore, principal at Moore Architects, who was retained to design the expansion with lead architect Jill Gilliand, along with interior designer Liz Mearns of Imagine Design.

In addition to increasing the home's square footage and incorporating two extra bedrooms, the design team also included a traditional front porch in the renovation, as well as several custom components, like a floating TV wall with bookshelves on either side, an extra-long window seat in the living room, and cushioned built-in reading nooks on the second-floor landing.

"We also created a direct spatial relationship between the inside and outside," says Charles. "By leveling the exterior grading, we added a screened porch off the dining room, creating an L-shape; in its elbow, we designed an expansive outdoor stone terrace." Then, Liz thoughtfully furnished the area for alfresco dining and lounging.

Although the homeowners have an extensive collection of McCarty Pottery and several antique rugs, they wanted the house to be mostly furnished afresh.

"We went with a mix of current and traditional styles to create an eclectic, collected vibe in the home," says Liz. "Though our palette was neutral, we did select fun patterned fabrics to bring more color and whimsy into the space."

For example, in the dining room, chairbacks are upholstered in a bold, contemporary botanical textile, and the modern trellis-pattern rug defining the living room's footprint is in a washed indigo. Throw pillows on the window seat continue the pattern play and make the spot an inviting nook for lounging.

"For the kitchen, we selected crisp white Shaker-style cabinetry and contrasting black counters but warmed the island up with a walnut butcher-block top," says Liz.

The kitchen is adjacent to the dining room that opens onto the new screened porch. With its fireplace and TV wall and vaulted shiplap ceiling with a central fan, this outdoor space is also suitable for year-round use. "The look here is more California contemporary—it's quiet, neutral, and textural," adds Liz.

The kitchen features Shaker-style cabinets with polished nickel pulls and knobs, as well as an apron-front farmhouse sink. The thick walnut countertop on the island and an antique runner add warmth to the space.

The home office has a moody palette. A thoughtful selection of vintage furnishings, including an oak desk and chair, makes this space feel cozy and collected.

The primary bedroom was designed around artwork depicting a street scene in Paris, which was created by the wife's French grandmother who met her GI husband after WWII.

"I'm always inspired by items that tell my clients' stories; I find that the most poignant stories become prominent in our finished design," Liz says.

Hence, the artwork and the vintage rug take center stage in the bedroom, while the upholstered bed and neutral furnishings combine to create an atmosphere of calm.

One of the beloved retreats in the house has become the second-floor landing's oversize window seats beneath the eaves and centered by a tiered rattan chandelier overhead. Each seat has a custom cushion and wall-mounted sconces for night reading.

"The house is already perched on its hill, overlooking the street, but these spots create secret hideaways with a view to the world below," says architect Jill.

When all is said and done, the cottage-style house definitely became larger but still lives in ways small and charming.

This is one of two window seats built into the eaves on the second floor. A patterned wallpaper and sconces add interest and light to the spot, which is furnished with a custom cushion and medley of pillows.

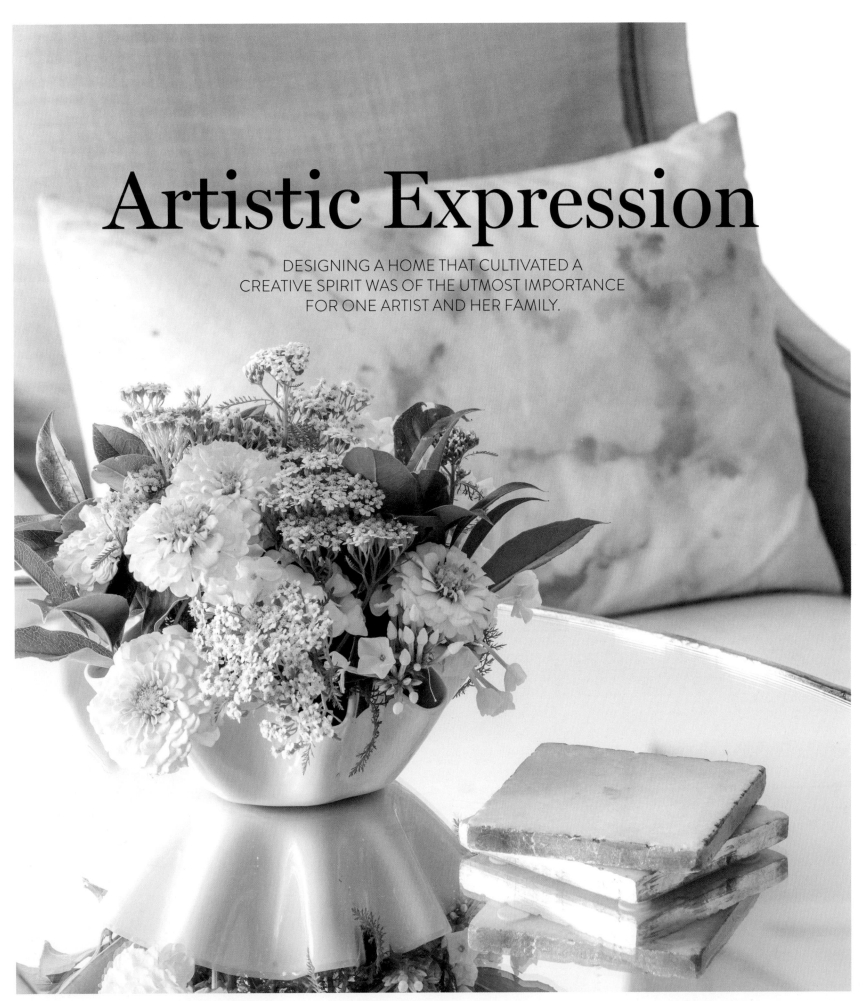

Artistic Expression

DESIGNING A HOME THAT CULTIVATED A
CREATIVE SPIRIT WAS OF THE UTMOST IMPORTANCE
FOR ONE ARTIST AND HER FAMILY.

When it came time for Birmingham, Alabama, artist Susan Gordon and her husband to trade their bungalow for a house more suitable to their growing family, Susan knew that, rather than buy a finished home, she wanted something she could put her unique mark on. "We were trying to find basically the ugliest house on a good lot on a good street so we could redo it because I knew I would want to buy a house and make it mine," she says.

Once they found it, Susan, with the help of Willow Homes, worked her magic. The addition of an extra bedroom and bathroom provided needed space, and a rework of the layout created an openness between the living room and kitchen, which was relocated to the front corner of the home. "I knew I wanted the kitchen in a light-filled space," Susan says, explaining that, since the home is located on a cul-de-sac, they wanted to have the main living areas placed where they could watch the neighborhood children playing.

When it came to color, Susan's passion for art influenced her decision to encase the design in a neutral palette warmed by layered textures. "I wanted it to feel like a blank canvas but with an element of feeling homey and cozy as well," she says. The choice showcases a collection of original artwork—a big priority for the design—as well as pieces by her own company, Susan Gordon Pottery, LLC. Throughout the space, a smattering of colorful accents reflects the style she injects into her own work, painting the space with broad strokes of cheerfulness.

The subdued but nature-inspired color palette allows the items Susan had on her checklist for the renovation, like the shiplap ceiling detail over the dining room table, to truly shine. "I had some ideas for the house I definitely wanted to execute, but I'm not a homebuilder or an interior designer, so I definitely needed the help to execute them," she says.

Katherine Bailey of Willow Homes, as well as the designers at Hartman Neely Interiors, assisted Susan in creating the look she wanted, which involved a mixture of classic and contemporary pieces to create something fresh but timeless—as in the small den, where the family

spends most of their time. "I definitely didn't want [the design] to feel like a snapshot of one moment in time, in terms of what was the most stylish thing in that moment," she says. "I wanted it to be something that I would enjoy for decades."

As in the rest of the home, the den spills over with timeless touches, like the built-in bookshelves and tufted sofa that make it the perfect place for movie and game nights. Hung against walls painted a moody blue-black, a piece by artist Holly Addi is an eye-catching representation of the underlying passion that informed parts of the design process.

"When you buy a piece of art, you buy a piece of that artist. . . . You really fall in love with them and who they are and what they're doing," Susan says. "And so, first and foremost, I like to buy art from people I admire." And while there are still plenty of names Susan would love to add to her walls, her existing collection is the perfect finishing touch on a home built around a love of creative expression.

"I knew I wanted something kind of moody and romantic in the bedroom," Susan says, pointing out the deep-hued accent wall that backs the iron bed. She carried the dramatic touch over to the slim set of barn doors that frame the entry to the primary bathroom.

COASTAL COTTAGES

FROM OCEANFRONT NEIGHBORHOODS TO LAKESIDE LIVING, OUR COASTAL COTTAGES ARE LAYERED WITH DESIGN INSPIRATION THAT CELEBRATES COLOR AND STYLE BY THE WATER.

Waterfront Idyll

COASTAL COTTAGE DÉCOR MAKES FOR
COMFY FAMILY GATHERINGS.

"Like everything else on the Eastern Shore, it was the waterfront views and relaxing lifestyle that initially attracted our clients to the area," says interior designer Jamie Merida of Jamie Merida Interiors, who worked on this Harris Creek property in Sherwood, Maryland, with lead designer Carol Wheeler.

The homeowners—a retired husband and wife—bought the three-bedroom house in 2019, adding the pool house one year later during the pandemic.

"We'd been renting in the area for several years," says the wife. "My husband is an avid fisherman and kept a boat in a nearby marina. When we decided to purchase a second home, we fell in love with the views and seclusion afforded by this property."

The other big attraction was that the house had been maintained in pristine condition. Other than constructing the pool house, all other changes would be largely cosmetic—paint and furnishings.

The cottage-style home also had an enticing open floor plan, encompassing a kitchen as well as dining and living areas with glass windows and doors taking advantage of the waterfront scenery.

"Our primary house is an 1813 log cabin filled with rustic antiques. That wasn't going to work down here," says the wife. "We wanted something completely new and fresh, coastal and comfortable. My only requirement was to use durable furnishings because we intended to use the house as a gathering place for family—we have two grown sons and three granddaughters."

The slate was clean for the design team, who began with nothing but "a folding table and two camping chairs, probably relegated to the garage," recalls Carol.

The residence now has a transitional coastal style. Comfortable sofas covered in performance fabrics and accent furnishings in woven natural textures create a relaxed ambience. The palette consists of neutrals and a range of blues that don't compete with the views. Patterns play with sea-inspired elements, from fish prints to nautical stripes.

"In the layout, we made sure there were lots of places to gather," says Jamie, noting the different seating and dining options scattered throughout the main spaces. "Whether playing a board game in the sunroom, snacking at the kitchen island, or hanging out en masse in the living room, there are plenty of options."

THE VELVETEEN RABBIT

He said, "You become. It take
a long time. That's why it doesn't
happen often to people who brea
easily, or have sharp edges, or wh
have to be carefully kept. Generally
by the time you are Real, most o
your hair has been loved off, and yo
eyes drop out and you get loose in
the joints and very shabby. But thes
things don't matter at all, because onc
you are Real yon can't be ugly, excep
to people who don't understand."

44.

The pool house, designed by architect Charles Paul Goebel and built by Gary Smith Builders, not only added 900 square feet to the property but also increased entertainment areas, with a dining room that opens poolside and features an 8-foot-long dining table surrounded by rattan-and-vinyl chairs and lit overhead by a pair of spherical rattan chandeliers hanging from a vaulted, sky blue ceiling.

"The pool house furniture, including the indoor-outdoor sofas, are all pieces that can stand up to wet bathing suits," says Carol.

The homeowners were also intent on using local sources for the home's interiors. The cherry wood dining furniture and kitchen stools were made by local craftsmen, and a lot of the art was sourced from nearby Easton, Maryland, galleries.

"Whether it's me with my girlfriends or my husband on a fishing trip, we love spending time down here," says the wife. "It's also become a great place for our family to meet. We love getting together to enjoy the Eastern Shore."

Sunroom furnishings include a duo of textured woven armchairs paired with a sofa atop an indoor-outdoor rug. This relaxing space also features a dining table and chairs, providing a spot to enjoy a board game or jigsaw puzzle.

The pool house bedroom touts beaded board walls and a vaulted ceiling. The blue-and-white palette continues from the art to the bedside chest, and the printed bedding imparts a decidedly tropical feel.

Home in the Hamptons

DESIGNING A CALMING RETREAT FROM THE HECTIC LIFESTYLE OF MANHATTAN,
INTERIOR DESIGNER JOSHUA SMITH HELPED THESE STYLISH HOMEOWNERS
CRAFT A COMFORTABLE YET CHIC GETAWAY.

DESIGN IN THE HAMPTONS

PENNOYER
RIDDER   A HOUSE in the COUNTRY   VENDOME

While this charming upscale cottage may reside in the Hamptons area on Long Island, New York, it strays from the typical coastal aesthetic. The Bridgehampton neighborhood provides more of a luxurious countryside feel, so when it came time to redesign this 1990s build, designer Joshua Smith and his team crafted a personalized country-coastal escape for homeowners Doug Eichman and Michael Yount.

This spirited and stylish couple have been together for more than 40 years, and together, they built and decorated their home but never felt as though it was quite finished. "They were in desperate need of a full refresh to make this home a comfortable place that reflected their personal styles," Joshua says. "Without compromising style, we decided to keep all of the clients' original furniture to be more sustainable. The pieces were reupholstered and reimagined—from replacing legs to skirting chairs and more." Reupholstering old furniture pieces with different fabrics can have a major impact on the mood of the room through color and pattern changes.

Doug and Michael's main request was to avoid plain, unadorned walls by making some bold statements, as well as incorporating wallpapers and patterns, while maintaining a timeless feel where they and their guests can relax and be themselves in this space. Joshua found inspiration in his garden, and delicate florals became the muse of this cottage refresh. "I became enamored with peonies. Their gentle, beautiful vibrancy spoke to me, and I've been waiting for the chance to incorporate that into one of my designs," he says. "Luckily, this project provided the perfect chance to bring that natural beauty indoors in a unique way."

The main color thread throughout the first floor is a striking magenta—or "peony pink" as Joshua calls it. "It started with the wall covering from Phillip Jeffries in the powder room, which is always the perfect place to go bold," he says. "Then, we chose to carry that buzzing energy into the back of bookcases with the shade Peony by Benjamin Moore—it couldn't be more perfect." And the Turkish rug for the foyer had amazing magenta and earth tones to round out the palette.

As you step inside the gracious entryway, the newly added millwork creates architectural interest without breaking the bank. Joshua shares, "There was way too much plain Sheetrock, and the simple addition of the wood detail up-leveled this space big time."

Designer Joshua Smith carries a common colorway throughout the entire home. "Magenta was my thread, and a powder room is a chance to go big or go home," Joshua shares. "Since it's visited for short intervals, you can be more spirited with choices—so here, we wanted a jewel box, and I think we did it!"

Joshua found creative ways to thoughtfully add color, pattern, and texture throughout the home. "Without texture, a room will feel flat. It's probably the most important layer one can give to a space," he says. "Whether it is a monochromatic scheme or complementary scheme with multiple colors, without various textures, you end up with boring."

A charming vestibule connecting the foyer to the formal living room becomes a statement that draws guests further inside thanks to the creative usage of a Schumacher grass cloth wall covering. "I wanted it to feel like a decorated tunnel, and when you got to the other side, you get the big reveal," Joshua says. "It's an unexpected surprise."

The formal living room is an ideal place to enjoy morning coffee or a late afternoon cocktail hour, especially when guests are visiting. A personal charm is found amongst the homeowners' collections, and the warmth of the fireside is highlighted with playful design elements and vibrant hues. "The personality you're surrounded with in the bookcases makes the space playful and fun," Joshua says. "The clients love color, but I was careful not to overdose on it, as you might get sick of it in two years."

The open-concept living and dining rooms flow seamlessly together along the back of the house. The use of drapery fabric from Kravet helps maintain a visual connection and provides just the right dressiness needed to keep the magenta thread running throughout the space. Both areas have French doors opening out to the back porch boasting lush verdant views of the pool just beyond.

The cozy living area is thoughtfully designed for comfort without compromising on style. Joshua incorporated plush furnishings so Doug and Michael can easily relax and enjoy watching television, while a Louis Vuitton trunk serves as a coffee table adding an unexpected, upscale edge to the décor.

The lively couple entertains often, so Joshua helped them create a dining area that feels casual and comfortable for guests. "We wanted to keep things light," he says, noting they didn't want it to feel overly formal. Old furnishings found a fresh life thanks to new fabric choices, and a merry mix of antiques gives the rooms a storied interest. "I love mixing vintage and antique with new because of its sustainability and stylishness," Joshua says. "The thrill of combining these items is incorporating modern pieces into more traditional spaces or vice versa. It provides a stunning juxtaposition that veers you away from a 'catalog look,' creating a more livable interior. It's a chance to incorporate one's unique personality into the space."

The cottage kitchen received a face-lift with painted blue cabinets and a new glass tile backsplash, which has a green undertone to it that helps bring the outdoors in. "It really gave this room personality and charm; it now feels like it has a quiet confidence," Joshua says. "My first job before going out on my own was for Steven Gambrel, and he once said, 'Throw in just a little clash, and you'll make the room more interesting,' so that's what I did here! It's a good way to avoid a very 'matchy-matchy' look."

Joshua shares that the key to successful design when mixing vintage or antique pieces with brand-new elements is balance. "Be wary of mixing too many periods and styles in one room—it confuses the space's energy," he says. "Consider common threads between the objects like color, texture, and shape. Modern, clean lines always look great with antique furniture."

The four bedrooms allow for easy hosting with ample space for guests. "It's the perfect weekend getaway from the hectic city of New York," Joshua says. "You really do want to kick off your shoes, grab a book, and just settle in. Each bedroom has its own personality, so guests feel like they are in a five-star bed-and-breakfast."

The design goal for the primary bedroom was complexity without sacrificing serenity. By keeping the tones muted, nothing is overpowering, even though there is abundant visual interest. "Harmony is crafted by mixing various pattern sizes and textures," Joshua says. The en suite bath is decked in cottage charm. Between the pin-striped wall covering and the creamy beaded board—this space is full of thoughtful details. Considering the space's smaller footprint, Joshua and his team elevated the experience with the touch of striped wallpaper, which makes the ceiling appear higher. And again, Michael and Doug's desire to eliminate the look of plain drywall throughout their home allowed for another opportunity to use all sorts of fun wallpapers. The color and texture continue in the other three guest rooms, which each have their own unique character yet feel connected to the home's overall design.

There's no shortage of comfort or style for overnight guests as they have their choice of darling accommodations. The wall covering in Jasper by Michael Smith adds loads of personality to this sweet retreat. Opposite: Joshua says that stripes and florals always go together, but the key is to find patterns that you love in colors you won't get tired of. "Part of the fun is doing the homework before the actual designing ever takes place. I love a blank canvas; it's pure potentiality," he says.

The coastal cottage's Cape-style architecture, with its cedar shingles and gorgeous turret, feels like the home has been there for ages even though it was built in the '90s. "I always love to give new homes instant personality and wisdom from perceived age," Joshua says. "When designing, I strive for livable beauty—meaning you're surrounded by beauty, but nothing is ornate, too precious, or opulent. My clients want homes where guests come in and feel comfortable, can sit back, relax, and enjoy a glass of wine without having to be overly concerned with the delicateness of everything." And it's clear that in this dreamy Hamptons retreat, he's achieved exactly that.

Doug and Michael have ample outdoor space for entertaining and relaxing. The back porch offers an extension of both the living and dining areas, while a charming stone path leads to an idyllic summertime oasis, complete with a pool house.

Stargazer Cottage

AFTER AN UNEXPECTED ENCOUNTER AND A
YEAR OF HARD WORK, THIS COUPLE CREATED
A LAKESIDE HAVEN WORTH COMING BACK TO.

While a rainy day at the lake may mean disappointment for most, for interior designer Kelly Kole and her husband, a bit of bad weather led to something life-changing. During a visit to a friend's home on Lake Santeetlah in North Carolina, the couple had a chance encounter that changed everything. "One rainy day, my friend said, 'Let's go look at houses just for fun,'" says Kelly. They went along with the whim and, by the end of the day, had found the home that would become their new summer haven.

What followed was a year of renovations, during which they gutted the home and reworked the layout for functionality. And with a year to make decisions about finishes and fixtures, Kelly had plenty of time to try something new. "For the first time in my life, I decided to go all neutral, which is very unlike me," she says, noting that the space was "a great laboratory," and that she found inspiration in the home's natural surroundings.

Despite not having worked with an all-neutral design before, Kelly knew how important it was to create interest within the space. To introduce color and texture, she pulled in vintage Turkish rugs, globally sourced textiles, and intentional art choices in every room. Throw pillows repurposed from Indian kantha quilts dot the family room sectional, and a cozy fireplace area was built around a painting commissioned from an Atlanta, Georgia, artist.

In the dining room, window treatments by Lacefield Designs feature a floral pattern atop a striking black background—a motif that reminded designer Kelly Kole of a local farmers' market she frequents while at the lake house. The fabric pulls in the black wicker chairs at each end of the farmhouse-style table, providing a sophisticated contrast to the softer finish of the Louis XVI-style chairs lining the sides.

The commissioned artwork over the fireplace, around which the structure was designed, is flanked by sconces Kelly had custom made by a couple in Tennessee. "[That painting] was really my pride and joy," she says. "It was kind of the kickoff to how I felt about the whole house."

Warm beams and other wood accents lead up to the centerpiece of the open layout—a kitchen of custom-made cabinets stained a warm brown with, as Kelly says, "a hint of gray." She adds, "It's such a tiny kitchen, and that really made the space." Kelly took the subway tile, paired with a dark brown grout, to the ceiling, topping off the look with live-edge wood shelves and pendant lights inspired by old train depots.

At the end of a day spent socializing in the open living space, the bedrooms offer quiet respite—and plenty of cozy style. More kantha quilts paired with Anthropologie pillows warm up a pair of beds in one guest room, while the other room features a calmer palette, finding its interest in a vintage rug and a macramé wall hanging from Guatemala.

A showpiece in the kitchen area, the collection of antique breadboards was inspired by a café in Charleston, South Carolina. "I made it my mission to collect those boards," Kelly says, noting that most of them are from France and Hungary. "I'm still growing the collection a little bit, but it is definitely the highlight of the kitchen."

"I wasn't sure if I was going to do window treatments in this house, because it's so pretty with the shiplap and all the light," Kelly says while pointing out the drapes in the primary bedroom. When she came across this pattern by Lacefield Designs, however, she was struck with the impression of sunlight on the water. "It was such a unique pattern that I said, 'That's it—I'm doing window treatments.'"

And while the inside of the house is welcoming and cozy, the outdoors are the main attraction. "This lake is really a hidden gem," Kelly says. With double porches perfect for everything from morning coffee to evening cocktails and an extra-large dock that encourages plenty of waterside activities, there's no shortage of opportunities for soaking up the sun—but the beauty doesn't disappear at sundown.

"When my husband would visit the home during construction . . . we had this rickety little dock at the time," says Kelly. "And he would go out at night and lay on his back and look up at the sky and call me and say, 'I've never seen stars like this in my entire life.'" The experience earned the home the name "Stargazer" and set the tone for a haven that would keep the Koles coming back every weekend of the summer—rain or shine.

Coastal Retreat

THOUGHTFUL DESIGN ELEMENTS
RESULT IN BEACH HOUSE BLISS.

When this North Carolina family was ready to dream up a vacation home on the coast, they found their ideal haven on beautiful Bald Head Island. The family called on the expertise of the builders at Whitney Blair Custom Homes, architects at Allison Ramsey out of Beaufort, South Carolina, and interior designers Vicky Serany and Kayla Boyle of Southern Studio Interior Design based in Cary, North Carolina. Together, this dream team of design experts created a cottage-style getaway decked out in coastal charm.

Bald Head Island is a tranquil sanctuary, located just south of North Carolina's Outer Banks, and is accessible only by ferry. Once you're there, the only transportation options are golf carts and bicycles, which simply enhances the appeal of the destination. "That's the charm of the island," Vicky says. "[The homeowners] are there for entertaining and creating memories with family and friends on the coast. It's your classic get-away-from-it-all beach house."

Since this is a second home, the family opted for design choices that felt a bit more playful than their more traditional primary residence. "It's casually sophisticated," Vicky says of the overall design. "The goal was fresh and fun!"

As you step through the front door, you'll discover a rich palette of vibrant colors that reflect the coastal surroundings, like deep ocean blues and sparkling sea greens. Though the home's square footage is small, thoughtful design choices helped to make it feel and appear more spacious than it is. "We really paid attention to the size and scale of the furniture, so a small space lives much larger," Vicky says.

Guests enter the home through the dining area. Vicky and Kayla worked closely with the homeowners and selected a round table to best utilize the space. "It's a tight space, but the round table allows easier access to maneuver around," Vicky says. "We added those fun chairs with the white finish to keep it light and bright and fresh but still have an edge." The dining area connects to the kitchen and is open to the living area as well.

The cottage kitchen marries important entertaining elements like a large island and ample storage and cooking space with contemporary design. "The homeowners had a clear vision—[they] wanted something a little bit fresh and different but not too out there," Vicky says. So together, they selected a deep blue hue for the bottom cabinets, island, and wet bar, and added brass hardware to balance the otherwise all-white kitchen.

The home was completed just before the pandemic began and made for an ideal retreat for the family's high school- and college-age children while schools were closed. The living room sofas and teal accent chairs from LEE Industries provide the perfect place to relax.

Custom window treatments in a coral-patterned fabric from Thibaut add a striking touch of blue color that is visible throughout the open-concept dining and living areas. "The homeowners have fabulous taste!" Vicky says.

The rattan finish on the counter stools from Serena & Lily gives the kitchen a contemporary, coastal flair. The brass end caps on the chair legs thoughtfully mirror the pulls and pendant lights.

Upstairs, a cozy loft serves as a perfect landing for watching TV or reading books after a morning walk on the shore and for playing games with friends in the evening. "Literally every square inch of that space is maximized," Vicky shares. They paired practicality with the pretty design elements by incorporating C-tables for sleek, slim surfaces and little stools that can double as extra seating if needed.

The primary suite and three comfortable guest bedrooms each pack a punch of summer color and beckon sweet island dreams. A bunk room with four twin-size beds allows ample space for extra guests. The blue-painted bunks pop against the shiplap and lead to the upper porch at the end of the hallway.

This charming guest room is sweetly serene. A curved rattan bed from Anthropologie anchors the space, and a custom bolster pillow and matching window treatment in fabric by Laura Park add the perfect pop of color.

Outside, the home has multiple porches, both upstairs and downstairs. Vicky and Kayla created several outdoor seating areas and even included a cozy picnic area for the family to enjoy dining together while soaking in the ocean breeze.

"We work in the primary home market a lot, but our second home market is so much fun. People are happier at the beach," Vicky says. "It's when you're away from work, and you have time with your family; you're having that extra cup of coffee in the morning, and you have time to cook and make pancakes and sit around having conversations. You don't always have that during our busy lives at home, so that's what we try to create for people—happy spaces for family."

COUNTRY COTTAGES

FROM MODERN FARMHOUSES TO RUSTIC RETREATS, OUR COUNTRY
COTTAGES ARE PACKED WITH PERSONALITY AND STORIES OF
STYLISH DECORATING WITH COMFORTABLE INTERIORS.

Heartfelt Haven

A LIFELONG LOVER OF ANTIQUES FILLS HER TEXAS BUNGALOW AND
DISTINCTIVE OUTDOOR SPACES WITH CHERISHED PIECES PASSED DOWN AND
PASSIONATELY COLLECTED, CRAFTED, AND CURATED ACROSS DECADES.

When Patty and Scott Herron came across the early 1900s cottage in La Grange, Texas, that would become theirs, Patty's father recalled fond childhood memories of daily strolls by the home as he walked to school. They purchased it in 1995, and as Patty began the process of furnishing and decorating—one that continues today—it was only fitting that she started with family pieces, the foundation of her thoughtfully collected aesthetic made up of gathered vintage charm and creative heartfelt presentations.

"It all started with getting hand-me-down furniture and décor from my parents, grandparents, and great-aunties," Patty says. "We're talking things that were stored in one of the barns on my daddy's farm. I've just built on that. Decorating has been a continuous process since we moved in. . . . My love has always been antiques and vintage, mixed with some new pieces, to create unique comfort."

After a year in the home, their daughter, Abby, was born, and desiring more space, they built an addition about the size of the original house while maintaining the exterior's Craftsman-style influence and the historic integrity of the interiors. "We love that it is an older home with character like original wood plank walls, wood flooring and windows, and a pedestal tub," Patty says. "Antique and vintage furnishings and décor look perfectly at home here. It's quaint, cozy, and welcoming."

In the mudroom area, homeowner Patty Herron shows off vintage collections amid coordinating fixtures, such as her grandfather's tool trug that houses her breadboards. For the stairway gallery, she compiled antique oil paintings and mismatched whitewashed frames and hung them with ribbon. "Those old original stairs and wood wall were just one of the reasons I fell in love with our house," she says.

The galley kitchen utilizes a mix of covered and glass-front cabinets and open shelving to help strike a balance between creating display space for the pieces Patty cherishes while also keeping clutter to a minimum in the narrow room.

Patty explains the dwelling's look as an eclectic mix of similar vintage styles. "I half kiddingly, half seriously describe my overall vibe as French brocante, rustic farmhouse, romantic prairie, and cottage with a bit of glam," she says. Over time, the home has become a treasure trove of beloved collections, patiently sought after and resourcefully displayed in reclaimed furnishings, often pieces Patty has created by combining finds to suit her needs.

Kitchenware collections abound, spanning old wooden breadboards, green canning jars, white café au lait bowls, aqua transferware, and an abundance of ironstone. "There is something about stacks of ironstone that makes my heart pitter-patter," Patty says. Her latest hunt has been for French tureens, which she currently displays in a fixture she crafted by stacking a white salvaged case atop a wooden chest.

Throughout the home, groupings of antique mirrors—from beveled to scalloped piecrust varieties—add light and depth to many spaces, and mismatched linens and cozy quilts soften the living areas and bedrooms.

La Grange, Texas, and other small neighboring towns like Round Top and Warrenton are known for their antiques stores and shows, offering a shopping mecca to scour for hidden gems that Patty has taken advantage of over the years—and still does today. "I'll think I have things exactly as I want, and then I add, take away, or change things," she says.

Everything adheres to a relatively neutral palette with pops of color that Patty changes with the seasons of both the calendar and life. She had always decorated with red, but when her dad passed away in 2015, she found it hard to live with the vibrant hue while she grieved.

During the 2020 pandemic, she decided she was ready to reintroduce her signature shade and skillfully applied dashes all around. "I fell in love with grain sacks and French ticking with red stripes," Patty says. "I built on that with old fabrics, linens, and quilts. The red livens things up and makes me happy."

The bedrooms are where Patty's signature color shines—in true vintage fashion, of course—from the toile quilt in the primary bedroom to a treasure trove of favorite finds in the guest room. "I showcase my love of red in this room with the bedding, vintage linens, and small touches," she says. She amplified the hue by bringing light and reflection to the space with assorted antique mirrors.

The Herrons' outdoor areas continue to evolve but remain seamless extensions of their home's interiors—from the screened porch they added during their '90s renovation to the distinctive greenhouse they built in 2021. "I've always gardened and have dreamed of a greenhouse made from vintage windows," Patty says of the space she also uses as her she-shed.

Patty recently added a bucket list item to the exterior—a greenhouse made entirely of vintage windows. She found a source for most of the windows, drafted a design for their placement, and let Judy Kurtz of Bluebonnet Renovators bring her vision to life. "Her team was able to puzzle piece the windows and architectural salvage together from my sketches, and make my dreams come true," Patty says.

Though almost everything in her home is one of a kind, Patty says it's the way she presents her pieces, as well as the meaning behind them, that makes her cottage truly special. "I think my antique furniture, my collections, and how they are put together are definitely unique," she says. "I also think the love I feel for them makes it unique. In each room or area, I have pieces that have a family connection or remind me of items my mom or grandmas had. My vision has always been to have a home that people walk into and instantly feel like they've had a warm hug."

Creative Combinations

AFTER MOVING FROM TENNESSEE, THIS FAMILY OF FOUR IS LEAVING
THEIR MARK ON THE NEW HAMPSHIRE COUNTRYSIDE.

After a year of house hunting from their home in Nashville, Tennessee, it seemed as if the Mitchells wouldn't find what they were looking for. "I really wanted an antique home—at least 100 years old," says homeowner and owner of Home Glow Design, Amy Mitchell. But their search finally bore fruit when they discovered a 1790 Federal farmhouse in New Hampshire.

While the home was in good physical shape, it had seen several updates over the decades and lost some of its original charm. "It didn't have any personality left inside," says Amy. "And so, we moved in, in 2012, and basically started decorating and renovating about one room per year as our budget would allow." When it came to planning the overall design, Amy cites the words "charming," "fresh," and "classic" as guiding influences, noting the concept of combining timeless silhouettes with more updated twists.

"I've never tried to be authentic in this house," she explains, in part because the budget precluded a full-scale, true-to-period restoration. "So, I think that gave me some leeway in how I approached this, and it also allowed me to use things that are a little different." Beyond that, it encouraged the use of traditional lines made comfortable for the family's lifestyle. "Just adding a couple of [antique] pieces into a room gives it soul, gives it patina," she says. "You decorate a whole room with antiques, and all of a sudden, you're living in a museum piece, and nobody's comfortable anymore."

"Art is always a part of the design goal for me," Amy says. "My husband is very particular that everything that goes on our walls has a meaning . . . So, as I've designed each room, I have searched for the art at the same time."

One of Amy's goals with the design was to create, as she says, "implied layers of time," which came into play in the living and kitchen spaces. Faced with an awkward addition from the '70s, the Mitchells used a little imaginative thinking to craft the illusion of a former porch that was closed in and converted to a sitting area—which was a must-have on their list.

Achieving one goal, however, brought on a ripple effect of new challenges to resolve, including the realization that there would be no room for an island in the kitchen. "Not all kitchens need islands, and historically, the center table was very appropriate—it was used as both a

worktable and where people sat down to eat," Amy says. "So, that's what I decided to go with, and I thought that would really create great flow."

Adjustable pendant lights over the table facilitated its dual roles, but there was still the problem of reduced storage. "Every single cabinet is absolutely utilized," Amy says. Loving the look of stepback cupboards but unable to find an antique that would fit the space, she had her cabinetmaker create a furniture-look end cabinet in walnut to serve as a pantry and hub for small appliances. Even so, paring down was paramount. "We whittled down to those things that we really use; all of our day-to-day dishes are in that hanging plate rack unit," Amy says.

Opposite: Complementing the chandelier, a pair of pressed-glass lamps stand tall on the reproduction sideboard. Rather than seeking out matching stools in a barley twist or similar classic style, Amy accented the vignette with more contemporary ottomans—demonstrating her talent for blending old with new.

Along with two of the bedrooms and the library, Amy designed the dining room before she entered the world of professional decorating—which means she didn't yet have access to trade sources. Instead, she relied on her own ingenuity to find the perfect pieces, including a pressed-glass chandelier she got for a steal. "I could have switched that out at any time, but I think it's just so pretty," she says. She adds that she wanted her home to stand the test of time, rather than having to refresh things every few years, "so that it is the consistent backdrop of our memories."

Taking a break from the eye-catching wallpaper—but not from bold style overall—the library stands out because of the rich cobalt that coats it from ceiling to floor. The room takes its cues from the rug by the brick fireplace, which served as a springboard for the color palette of the entire home. "There was definitely a space-planning challenge," says Amy, who needed to fit a lot into the narrow chamber—including a baby grand piano and plenty of bookshelves.

Serving as a place for sons Earl and Lee to practice music, and for Amy and her husband, Rob, to unwind in the evenings, the room pops with contemporary elements couched in traditional shapes. "The sofas and one of the chairs have sort of a traditional English arm, which is an older style, but then I brought in those 1950s Murano red lamps to kind of shake it up," Amy says.

She paid no less attention to the more private spaces in the home, taking every detail into account. "You need to think about flow within a bedroom just as much as you would in a living room," she says. Considering storage, floor space, and the natural tendencies of the eye in traversing a room, she crafted a primary bedroom that would appeal equally to herself and her husband, Rob. A balance of masculine and feminine features blends beautifully atop the backdrop of a whimsy-filled forest print. "[Rob] actually saw that wallpaper in one of my magazines and absolutely loved it," Amy says.

While her oldest son's room has stood the test of time, with its blue pin-striped walls and rich wood furnishings, her youngest's boasts a bolder palette and more contemporary prints. Both, however, share common features. "I think a bedroom, no matter the size, needs to have a place to sit down that is not on the bed," Amy says—even if the space only allows for a chair or an end-of-bed bench. "For kids, I really try to have a desk or a place to work, and a bookshelf and dresser."

Starting with a space void of personality, Amy took great care in putting her family's unique mark on this historic farmhouse—all while celebrating the charms of timeworn style in comfort. And with every out-of-the-box design decision and creative combination, the Mitchells' New Hampshire home took on a life of its own.

The Mitchells' sons, Earl and Lee, each enjoy a distinct style in their respective spaces. While Lee's room is papered in an eye-catching print, Amy complemented the shade with more neutral blue accents, wooden finishes, and timeless stripes.

Country Refined

A NEW CONSTRUCTION IN RURAL PENNSYLVANIA DRAWS FROM ITS BEAUTIFUL BUCOLIC SETTING WITH SUBTLE, SOPHISTICATED INTERIOR DESIGNS THAT REFLECT THE HOME'S SURROUNDINGS RATHER THAN DISTRACT FROM THEM.

J ust outside of Allentown, Pennsylvania, a young, active family of five with a love of the outdoors and wide, open spaces found an idyllic location to create their own county retreat. They wanted a home that would be functional for life with children and stylish yet understated so the indoor spaces would seamlessly blend into expansive views of the property beyond. Overwhelmed with where to begin, they brought on designer Lisa Furey in the early stages to help achieve their vision.

"We took it from blueprint to accessories over the course of three years," Lisa says. "It's on a big, beautiful lot with a fishing pond and weeping willow trees. They are a warm and loving family—very close and very family oriented—and they are casual and wanted low maintenance. I saw a cozy, light and bright home where friends and family could gather for all sorts of occasions."

Starting at the structural level, Lisa worked with architect Christopher Carrigan of Historical Concepts to incorporate traditional farmhouse elements throughout, such as reclaimed wood beams, exposed brick, and shiplap, while upholding an aesthetic that was both refined and hard-wearing. "The shiplap on the walls was selected because it looks good, but more importantly, because it's protected," Lisa says of its sturdiness and painted satin finish that can be easily wiped down.

The wide-plank, distressed white oak flooring was chosen for similar reasons. "The lighter the floor, the less dirt it shows, and the more matte it is, the less scratches show," Lisa explains. "It's very family friendly." But it also serves as a beautiful base to the neutral color scheme that spans cool gray to warm brown interspersed with hushed blues and greens. "As a nature lover and minimalist at heart, I wanted to focus on the outdoors and take those colors inside," she says. "There is nothing bright or shiny—it is all textured and muted color."

With this emphasis on the scenery and thoughtful architectural foundation in place, Lisa approached the interiors with a careful finesse, filling the home with pieces that pointed back to these muses rather than pulling the spotlight from them. "We used mostly natural materials," she says. "I did not want it to look too new, though most pieces were. My selections were made based on function, durability, practicality, and, of course, looks. I wanted the outside to shine—the indoors played second fiddle—so selections feel quiet, and nothing screams, 'Look at me.'"

This begins in the airy, inviting entry, where many of the home's structural features, such as shiplap and exposed ceiling beams, are introduced alongside eye-catching organic fixtures like a bluestone tabletop. The foyer leads directly into a sprawling open-concept space that includes the living and dining areas, as well as the kitchen and a sunroom—all of which are backed with sizable windows and French doors that showcase the scenic surrounds.

In the living room, comfortable upholstery is swathed in subdued blues anchored by slightly masculine notes of dark gray and brown leather, which lend a rustic touch. The sunroom just beyond echoes the same palette with a fittingly lightened-up feel.

The kitchen finds distinction within the open floor plan with unexpected dashes of industrial style, such as a rolled steel range hood and metal seating, balanced by inclusions that instill vintage charm, like the dining area's dainty chandelier. The overall natural motif continues in brick accent walls, reclaimed wood open shelving, and an earthy olive green paint color on the cabinetry.

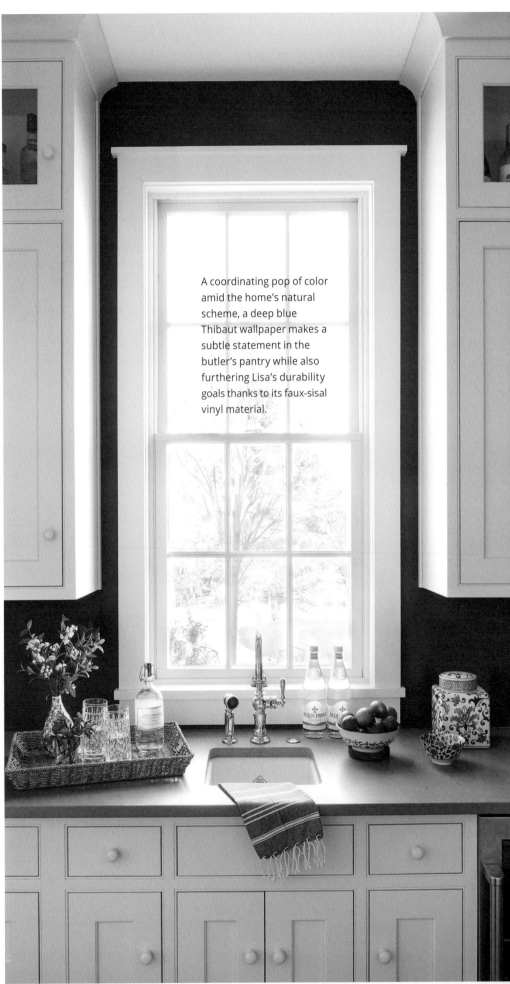

A coordinating pop of color amid the home's natural scheme, a deep blue Thibaut wallpaper makes a subtle statement in the butler's pantry while also furthering Lisa's durability goals thanks to its faux-sisal vinyl material.

Because the interiors were designed to take advantage of the exterior setting, Lisa describes this home as "indoor-outdoor," and the breezy sunroom captures that ideal perfectly as natural light floods the space, bouncing off of bright-white shiplap walls and a beaded board ceiling. A daybed draped in soft blue and cream linens adds to the dreamy aesthetic, while darker hues on woven furnishings and accents instill a grounding touch.

In the more utilitarian spaces, Lisa repeated many of the distinctive architectural features used throughout the rest of the cottage for continuity. In the mudroom, an exposed brick floor echoes accent walls seen elsewhere and offers a fitting drop zone for farmhouse comings and goings. She designed custom built-ins that harmonize in looks and provide functional storage between the mudroom and laundry room. Opposite: In the study, Lisa continued with shiplap walls but switched things up with a gray finish. A jib door leads to the primary bedroom for concealed convenience.

In the primary bedroom and bathroom, tranquil neutral tones gain interest and warmth from a rich mix of materials and textures, plus decorative details like artwork that reflects the country locale. "Some designers use a lot of bright colors and different fabrics and heavy draperies," Lisa says. "We did not need that because the outside is so pretty. The architecture and millwork are so perfect. We didn't need to distract from those things. We let them take front row."

And the result is exactly what they set out to accomplish—a dreamy family farmhouse that is "comfortable, durable, and fresh," as Lisa sums it up. "There's nothing fussy and nothing too dear. It's a warm and cozy country home."

Bucolic Delight

COLLECTED ANTIQUES FILL THIS TEXAS HOME WITH OLD MEMORIES, WHILE THE LAND INSPIRES PLENTY OF NEW ONES.

I dyllic memories of childhood days spent on her grandmother's farm fueled Jennifer Nicholas's longtime desire to create her own oasis in the Texas countryside—and a penchant for antiques and decorating inspired her to do so by restoring life to a timeworn farmhouse. "I had been looking for a couple of years," Jennifer says. So, when a property in the antiques destination of Round Top, Texas—just a short drive away from her home in Houston—came on the market, the decision was easy. "I just went ahead and bought it," she says.

With the purchase made, Jennifer and her husband, Jim, had their work more than cut out for them. The to-do list included adding a bathroom, insulating the walls, and replacing the roof—and if that wasn't enough of a challenge, the couple started by relocating the farmhouse to a new spot on the property to take better advantage of the lake view. "I'm not sure if I'll ever do it again," Jennifer says of the renovation, "but I took it on because I just wanted the experience of doing it—and I absolutely loved it."

Opposite: Jennifer says that the Brimfield Antiques Flea Market in Massachusetts is one of her favorite spots to find ironstone for her collection, which she displays in a hutch she kept in storage in anticipation of finding her farmhouse. On either side, metal sconces gifted by one of her children hold taper candles and add a dash of nature-inspired charm.

With new plumbing, flooring, and wall planking in place, Jennifer dove into the fun part: finding homes for all the antique pieces she'd gleaned from market vendors at Round Top over the years. An oversize hutch with decades of patina shows off a collection of ironstone pitchers, a chandelier made of antique spoons sparkles above the kitchen table, and a reclaimed barn door turned on its side creates a centerpiece on the living room wall—all adding layers of age and character atop the new siding and painted pine floors.

A creative twist turned the reclaimed barn door over the sofa into a personalized focal point. By turning it on its side, Jennifer highlighted the existing structural detailing with a nod to the family's last name: Nicholas.

An old armchair reupholstered in floral fabric that Jennifer already had provides a sweet spot to relax in the decidedly feminine pink bedroom.

Step into the bedrooms, however, and you'll get a closer look at the home's history, as elements like the powder pink beaded board walls remained untouched during the refresh. "I loved the way it looked," Jennifer says of the naturally weathered backdrop that beautifully sets the stage for a romantic assembly of vintage linens and bold florals. An antique awning adds a charming touch above the bathroom door, which is itself an antiques fair find. "I have a thing about doors and windows," Jennifer says. "If I can use anything old, that's what I like to do."

And if, at times, she encounters challenges in finding a spot for her timeworn pieces, Jennifer meets them with creative flexibility. A cabinet that seemed destined for the kitchen found its spot instead in the bathroom, next to a soaking tub that speaks of relaxing country getaways.

"I filled it with my favorite pitchers," Jennifer says, noting her favorite floral-patterned finds that create a multihued display behind the glass doors. "You would think you'd have it filled with towels and linens, but no—I changed it up a little."

While the antique treasures and serene comforts of the farmhouse's interiors are plentiful, the land itself has its own charms, and the Nicholases' family often comes out to experience them. Jennifer herself notes that she "practically lives" on the property now, but it's especially precious for her to help her grandchildren create their own childhood memories. "It's just a whole different way to enjoy your days," she says, citing full days spent without a single car passing by. "People say things feed your soul. . . . That's how this place feels to me."

Jennifer's love of vintage bedding and linens goes back to her days working in the antiques business. While white linen and monogrammed pieces are favorites, a look at the bedrooms makes it clear where her heart really lies. "I have a soft spot for quilts," she says. "I try to use them wherever I can."

An example of new construction that provides plenty of antique charm, the recently completed garden shed shows off old details like the door and windows. A brick porch is a picturesque home for collected watering cans and lovingly cultivated blooms.

The chicken coop on the property was made of wood from an old storage shed that Jennifer took apart and reassembled with help from family members. "That's one of my favorite things about the whole place," she says.

Making a House a Home

THIS COUPLE'S HEART FOR HOSPITALITY MEETS
FAMILY-FOCUSED DESIGN—ALL WHILE BLENDING THE
BEST OF FARMHOUSE AND CONTEMPORARY STYLES.

After tackling the countless decisions involved with the construction of their Magnolia, Texas, new build, Lydia and Brad Walker found themselves creatively spent. The couple sought the help of interior designer Ashley Moore of Moore House Interiors to furnish their space with the finishing touches needed to set a welcoming tone for their family's forever home.

"Lydia already had a lot of farmhouse elements picked out with the [architectural] selections of the home," says Ashley. "She just wanted it to feel elegant but still cozy, warm, and casual." The Walkers often host anywhere from 50 to 200 kids from their church youth group, making stylish durability key to the overall design.

In the living room, rustic wood beams highlight a vaulted ceiling and lend warmth to the light and airy aesthetic. Custom built-ins and shiplap painted a crisp white offer subtle contrast to the creamier tones of the walls and upholstered furnishings. The matte black finish of the chandelier and sconces corresponds to the hardware on the built-in cabinets and the coffee table's iron base.

Since Lydia likes over-the-top decorating for every holiday, Ashley opted to keep the palette primarily neutral, letting the chambray blue rug add a dash of color and playful pattern. A pair of chesterfield sofas utilizes a linen-like performance fabric for a polished yet laid-back look furthered by the variegated stripe of the swivel chairs.

The living room leads into a playroom for the couple's two daughters. A precious playhouse—complete with a window box—built into the wall serves as the focal point. Nestled in a tiny alcove, a delightful reading nook is made extra cozy with the addition of a custom seat cushion, pillows, and knitted throw.

In the center of the room, a small table serves as the perfect spot for crafting, while a plethora of storage makes putting toys away more manageable. "I think the key to making a playroom work—especially when you have that much open shelving—is baskets," says Ashley. When it came to styling the higher shelves, Ashley and her team brought depth and interest by layering vintage items, such as a shoe mold and baskets, among newer pieces.

A wall of windows floods the breakfast nook with an abundance of natural light, while the wood table exudes rich warmth. "Typically, my go-to is to do black chairs, but with the light fixture, it might make the space feel a little too heavy," says interior designer Ashley Moore. "Adding white makes it pop a bit and just feel so light and airy."

Storage is essential when it comes to a thoughtfully designed playroom, and because the space opens into the main living area, keeping an orderly appearance was imperative. While clear bins work great in pantries, Ashley recommends utilizing opaque options to make tidying up easier for kids—and parents. "Inevitably, whatever you do, kids are not going to be organized," she says. "When they're asked to pick up, everything just goes in a tote. Being able to get matching baskets to just kind of tuck the toys away at times when people come over is truly key." The window seat features a trio of lower drawers to provide additional storage.

The patterned tile, painted cabinets, and functional layout were handpicked by Lydia, who relied on Ashley's team to accessorize the laundry room space with woven shades and smaller décor items.

you are
home
to me

Form and function unite in the laundry room where cabinets painted a cheery robin's-egg blue pair with a lively gray-and-white patterned tile. An abundance of countertops and lower storage for rolling hampers makes sorting and folding laundry a breeze.

Glass doors separate the room used for homeschooling and the family room, offering a seamless transition from work to entertainment. For a cohesive look between the two spaces, Ashley drew from the classroom's blue armoire when selecting a rug and throw pillows to dress up the beige sectional. Woven shades enhance the room's casual, relaxed ambience.

The small black hutch was an Anthropologie find Lydia fell in love with, and its interior features light wood tones that blend well with the rest of the space. "I'm a big proponent of, if you find something that you love—whether your designer tells you to use it or not—go for it," says Ashley.

The blue-and-neutral scheme continues in the primary bedroom, where shiplap makes a reappearance. Antique brass sconces lend themselves to late-night reading as they add contemporary flair. The nightstands' subtle herringbone design echoes the brick of the fireplace while framed artwork and a single plant adorn the mantel. "I feel like the mantel is a statement in and of itself, so we didn't want to overdo it," Ashley notes. "It was just about making it feel simple, and I think that just adds to the coziness of the space."

When it came to creating their dream home, the Walkers needed a design that fit their various needs—from homeschooling to hospitality—all while capturing their personality. "They just wanted us to come in and make it feel completed and like it was their home," says Ashley.

RESOURCES

Editor: Katie Ellis
Art Director: Jodi Rankin Daniels
Copy Editor: Adrienne Davis

Cover: Photography by Jenifer McNeil Baker.

Introduction, 8–9: Text by Katie Ellis; photography by Robert Radifera.

CLASSIC COTTAGES, 10
Twist on Traditional Style, 12–23: Text by Katie Ellis; photography by Michael Hunter; interior designs by Kim Armstrong, Kim Armstrong Interior Design, *kimarmstronginteriordesign.com*, 214-500-0600.

Timeless Charm, 24–39: Text by Katie Ellis; photography by Brian Bieder; interior designs by Maggie Griffin, Maggie Griffin Design, *maggiegriffindesign.com*; architectural designs by Jack Davis, Jack Davis Architect, *jackdavisarchitect.com*, 404-237-2333.

A Personal Canvas, 40–53: Text by Elizabeth Czapski; photography by Jenifer McNeil Baker; interior designs by Emily Johnston Larkin, EJ Interiors, *ejinteriors.net*, 214-484-3570; renovation construction designs by Carol Gantt, Gantt Design, *ganttdesign.com*, 214-228-0139.

A Change of Space, 54–69: Text by Bethany Adams; photography by Heidi Harris; interior designs by Anna-Louise Wolfe, *annalouisewolfe.com*, 678-680-3309.

Well-Crafted Cottage, 70–83: Text and styling by Charlotte Safavi; photography by Robert Radifera; interior designs by Liz Mearns, Imagine Design, *lizmearns.com*.

Artistic Expression, 84–93: Text by Bethany Adams; photography by Mac Jamieson; styling by Courtni Bodiford; architectural and interior designs by Katherine Bailey, Willow Homes, *gowillowhomes.com*, 205-206-6121; additional interior designs by Hartman Neely Interiors, *hartmanneelyinteriors.com*.

COASTAL COTTAGES, 94
Waterfront Idyll, 96–109: Text and styling by Charlotte Safavi; photography by Robert Radifera; interior designs by Jamie Merida, Jamie Merida Interiors, *jamiemerida.com*, 410-819-8666.

Home in the Hamptons, 110–123: Text by Katie Ellis; photography by Read McKendree; interior designs by Joshua Smith, *joshuasmithinc.com*.

Stargazer Cottage, 124–135: Text by Bethany Adams; photography by Lauren Rubinstein; interior designs by Kelly Kole, Kandrac & Kole Interior Design, *kandrac-kole.com*, 770-514-9699; renovations by Kyle Garland, Robbinsville Custom Moulding, *custommoulding.com*, 828-346-6144.

Coastal Retreat, 136–145: Text by Katie Ellis; photography by Dustin Peck; interior designs by Vicky Serany and Kayla Boyle, Southern Studio Interior Design, *southernstudio.com*, 919-362-5143; built by Whitney Blair Custom Homes, *whitneyblair.com*, 910-575-4900; architectural designs by Allison Ramsey Architects, *allisonramseyarchitect.com*, 843-986-0559.

COUNTRY COTTAGES, 146
Heartfelt Haven, 148–163: Text by Elizabeth Czapski; photography by Michael Hunter.

Creative Combinations, 164–179: Text by Bethany Adams; photography by Eric Roth; interior designs by Amy Mitchell, Home Glow Design, *homeglowdesign.com*; cabinet designs by Lisa Muskat, LKM Design, *lkm-design.com*, 603-472-2925.

Country Refined, 180–191: Text by Elizabeth Czapski; photography by Rebecca McAlpin; interior designs by Lisa Furey, Lisa Furey Interiors, *lisafureyinteriors.com*, 610-389-5231; architectural designs by Christopher Carrigan, Historical Concepts, *historicalconcepts.com*, 678-325-6665; built by Keith Hoeing, Erwin Forrest Builders, *erwinforrest.com*, 484-571-9990.

Bucolic Delight, 192–203: Text by Bethany Adams; photography by Michael Hunter; styling by Amanda Barkley.

Making a House a Home, 204–215: Text by Holly Seng; photography by Grace Laird; interior designs by Ashley Moore, Moore House at Home, *moorehouseathome.com*, 346-215-1077; architectural designs by Mark W. Todd Architects, *mwtoddarch.com*, 281-363-2593; built by American Mustang Custom Homes, *americanmustangcustomhomes.com*, 281-960-4141.

Additional Photography Credits:
Page 2: Photography by Dustin Peck.
Pages 4–5: Photography by Rebecca McAlpin.
Page 6: Photography by Heidi Harris.
Page 10: Photography by Jenifer McNeil Baker.
Page 94: Photography by Robert Radifera.
Page 146: Photography by Michael Hunter.
Pages 178–179: Photography by Emily O'Brien.
Page 217: Photography by Eric Roth.
Pages 218–219: Photography by Jenifer McNeil Baker.
Page 220: Photography by Mac Jamieson.
Back Cover: (Top left, top center, bottom left) Photography by Heidi Harris. (Top right, middle right, bottom right) Photography by Michael Hunter. (Middle left, bottom center) Photography by Jenifer McNeil Baker.